INTER

MW00680763

Christmas Gems

Book 2

Arranged by Nancy Lau

A Note to Students

These Christmas solos were written to allow rich keys and lush chords to create a depth of harmonies not often heard in traditional Christmas carols. Expressive playing mixed with much feeling is greatly encouraged as you play these solos.

May they conjure up sentiment mixed with joyful and tender Christmas memories!

Nancy Lau

CONTENTS

We Wish You a Merry Christmas

Traditional English Carol

Moderately fast; with swing (♩ = 120)

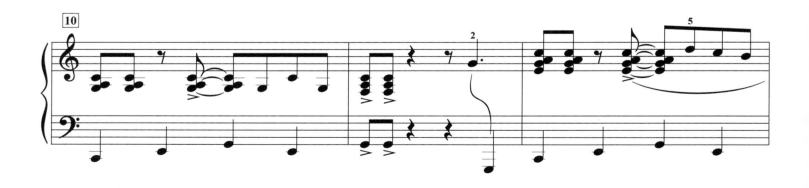

This arrangement © 2020 The FJH Music Company Inc. (ASCAP).
International Copyright Secured.   Made in U.S.A.   All Rights Reserved.

Andante espressivo (no swing) (♩ = ca. 84)

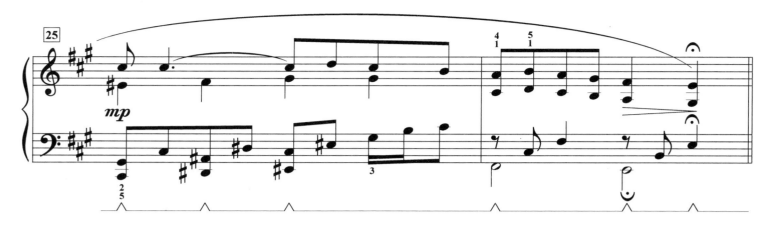

Tempo primo, with swing (♫ = ♩♪)

rit.   Mer - ry Christ - mas!   a tempo

Ukrainian Carol

Music and Words by
Mykola D. Leontovych

This arrangement © 2020 The FJH Music Company Inc. (ASCAP).
International Copyright Secured.   Made in U.S.A.   All Rights Reserved.   FJH2355

8

Silent Night

Words by Joseph Mohr
Music by Franz Gruber

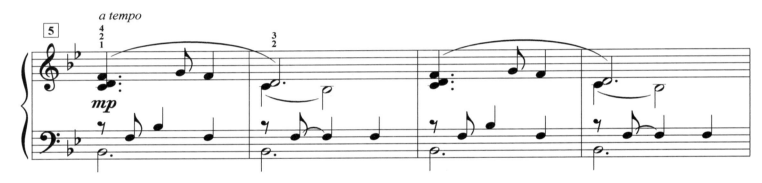

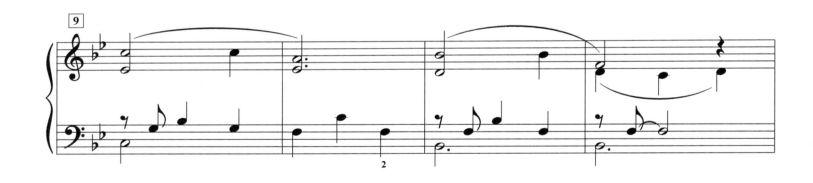

This arrangement © 2020 The FJH Music Company Inc. (ASCAP).
International Copyright Secured.   Made in U.S.A.   All Rights Reserved.

O Holy Night

Words translated by John S. Dwight
Music by Adolphe C. Adam

FJH2355

This arrangement © 2020 The FJH Music Company Inc. (ASCAP).
International Copyright Secured. **Made in U.S.A.** **All Rights Reserved.**

16

FJH2355

Ave Maria

Charles Gounod

Moderato; cantabile (♩ = ca. 80)

This arrangement © 2020 The FJH Music Company Inc. (ASCAP).
International Copyright Secured. **Made in U.S.A.** **All Rights Reserved.**

20

Away in a Manger

Words: Traditional
Music by James Ramsey Murray

This arrangement © 2020 The FJH Music Company Inc. (ASCAP).
International Copyright Secured.   Made in U.S.A.   All Rights Reserved.

22

FJH2355

Auld Lang Syne

Music: Traditional Scottish Melody
Words: Robert Burns

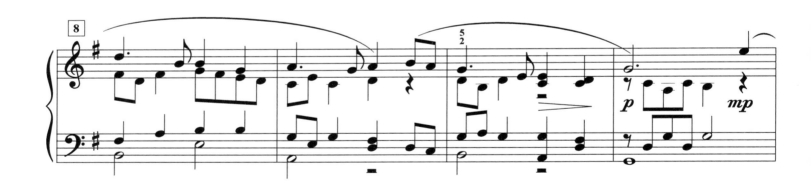

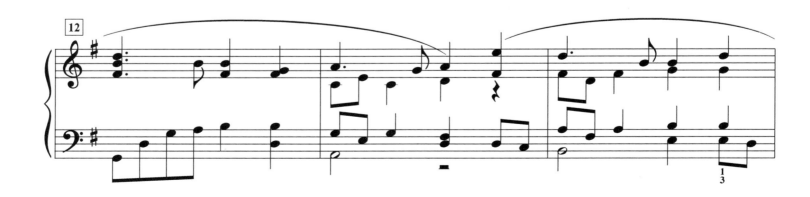

This arrangement © 2020 The FJH Music Company Inc. (ASCAP).
International Copyright Secured.   Made in U.S.A.   All Rights Reserved.